D0396656

Charlie's Monument

AN ALLEGORY OF LOVE

Blaine M. Yorgason

**Photography by
Alan B. Yorgason**

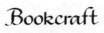
Bookcraft

Salt Lake City, Utah

Library of Congress Catalog Card Number: 79-56176
ISBN 0-88494-389-5

Second Edition

2nd Printing, 1980

Lithographed in the United States of America
PUBLISHERS PRESS
Salt Lake City, Utah

This is for you,
Charlie,
wherever you are

The Monument

God,
Before He sent His children to earth
Gave each of them
A very carefully selected package
Of problems.

These,
He promised, smiling,
Are yours alone. No one
Else may have the blessings
These problems will bring you.

And only you
Have the special talents and abilities
That will be needed
To make these problems
Your servants.

Now go down to your birth
And to your forgetfulness. Know that
I love you beyond measure.
These problems that I give you
Are a symbol of that love.

The monument you make of your life
With the help of your problems
Will be a symbol of your
Love for me,
Your Father.

Blaine M. Yorgason

CONTENTS

1

Charlie

Charlie's mother, when she first saw her little baby boy, held him close and cried just a tiny bit. No one, including the midwife who was there, was certain just why she cried. It may have been because of happiness, for now she at last had a child. And it may have been because of sadness: since her husband had died she had so wanted their only child to be a son who would be just like his father. But this little boy never could be like his father, for he was born with only one arm, and his legs and back were badly deformed and twisted.

Nevertheless, he was given the name of Charles Edward Langly, Jr. Maybe he would never look like his father, but he could be like him in other ways.

2

His mother knew, as she looked with love and sorrow upon her misshapen little Charles, that he would never live as other children did. And the question came then, unbidden: *God, why have you given him such a test?* Her heart groaned within her as she thought of his future, of the taunts of heedless children and the persecution of self-righteous adults who would feel that because he was not perfectly formed, neither could he be perfectly a man. She knew that she must never allow him to feel that because he was different he was not as good. She had to find a way to teach him self-confidence and the value of self-worth, for she knew that that was what her husband would have done. In fact, she could almost hear him saying to her that his son above all needed these two qualities, as well as the important attitude of love for others, if he was ever going to survive. And she vowed, then and there, that Charlie, with the aid of God and herself, would succeed.

It is never easy to learn new things, but for Charlie life seemed especially difficult. When other children his age were learning to walk he was still struggling to crawl. When Charlie had finally learned to use a sort of shuffle-kick method to move from one place to another, however slowly, all the other children were running here and there, playing childish games and shouting great shouts of joy in their unappreciated freedom.

Mrs. Langly ached with love and concern as she watched young Charlie grow, and though she never preached she was careful never to let a teaching moment pass unused.

3

For instance, Charlie would spend hours sitting near the gate listlessly drawing figures in the dust with his only hand while he watched the other children at play. One day as his mother walked past him on her way to the pump for water, Charlie looked up and asked in his innocent way, "Mom, why don't I have two arms like Joe and Billy and all the other kids?"

As she thought of what answer she could give him, she noticed the figure that Charlie had traced in the dust. Suddenly an idea came to her.

"Charles, tell me about your beautiful picture."

"Huh?"

"Tell me about the picture you drew there in the dust."

Charlie's eyes showed astonishment and pleasure as he looked from his mother to his drawing and back again, for he had no idea until then that he had really drawn a real picture.

"It's a deer," he said simply.

"Is that all?"

"Well, that's an Indian over there behind that rock, and this here line is an arrow he just shot, and it is going to hit the deer, and then he will have food for his family. He's the Daddy, you know."

"Yes he is, Charles, and that is a very good picture. How did you draw it?"

"With this here stick," Charlie replied proudly.

"Can you do another one?"

"Sure," he said, and all else was forgotten as he gripped the stick tightly in his hand and scratched another figure in the dust.

After he had finished and had explained the

second picture to his mother, she held out her hand to him and asked him to come inside.

When they were out of the hot desert sun she handed Charlie a cool glass of buttermilk and sat down on the doorbench beside him.

"Charles, you asked me why you have only one arm while all the other children have two. Of course I don't know for sure, but I would say that God gave you only one arm because that was all he felt you needed. Why, just now I watched you draw two fine pictures with your one hand, and I'd guess there aren't very many people with two hands that could do as well.

"Just remember, Charles, God never makes a mistake. He gave you all the abilities you'll ever need to become a real man."

Then Mrs. Langly got up and walked outside, wisely leaving Charlie alone to ponder her words. Somehow she seemed to know that Charlie was deciding then that there was really nothing he couldn't do, if he just worked at it.

There also came a day, a year or so later, when Mrs. Langly heard a shout from Charlie. Hastily abandoning the weeds in her small vegetable garden she rushed to the front of the house to find Charlie leaning against the doorframe, grinning happily as he drew in great gulps of air. There at his feet stood a pail of water, full almost to the brim.

"Look, Mom," he said proudly, "I carried it all the way and didn't spill a drop."

Mrs. Langly hugged Charlie to her while she spoke, tears of joy and pride streaming down her face.

"You see, Charles? God never does make a mistake. You can do anything you want to if you want to do it badly enough. And you can do it as well or better than anyone else. I knew you could, and now you know it too."

Another crisis was met by Charlie the day he first made his way to the one-room school at the other end of town. For weeks he had been looking forward to the beginning of school, for at last his mother had consented to let him go. But then, when it finally did start, Charlie was kept at home with a bad head cold. At last, a week later than everyone else, Charlie shuffled out the door with his broken slate and his lunch bag clutched tightly in his hand, whistling a happy song of anticipation as he went.

All day long Mrs. Langly fretted around the small home, forcing herself not to think about what might be happening to her little son. But then, late that afternoon, when her misshapen little boy came into sight, her worst fears were realized. His clothes were tattered and torn, his one hand was bruised and swollen, and a mixture of tears and blood had streaked the dust that covered his face.

Saying not a word she set about cleaning him up, desperately trying to ignore the occasional choking sobs that wracked his small body. Oh, how she wanted to hold him close to her and suf-

7

fer for him, and yet she somehow knew that for growth to come he must learn to stand alone.

For some time Charlie remained silent, but at last he was able to speak.

"Mom," and he seemed to whimper just a little as he asked it, "why did they hurt me? I did nothing to them, but they waited for me down by the creek after school, and I couldn't get away."

Charlie paused for a long moment as if in thought, then fiercely snarled, "But I'll get 'em! You bet I will!" Then again he began to sob.

Mrs. Langly stroked his hair as she silently prayed for wisdom to help her son past this most recent obstacle. *Oh, God,* she prayed, *what can I say to him? Please, tell me what to say.*

Then, as Charlie's sobbing slowly diminished, she began to tell him a story. This story had grown more real to her over the years, for it was of a boy who had grown up different from other children and who was teased and persecuted because of his differences. As she talked softly on about this other youth she became aware of a quietness creeping over her son. She told him of how this other man had stood alone, helping others with no thought of reward, all his life. At last even his few friends had abandoned him so that, alone, he was lifted up on a cross between two thieves and crucified for the sins of the world.

And as his mother spoke Charlie could imagine the peace and confidence that radiated from the face of this man who had been so troubled by the smallness of others. And Charlie decided that he too would overcome.

"Charlie," she said at length, "I suppose there are lots of people around who are not so blessed with love as you and He have been. They are afraid of what they don't understand, and in their fear they sometimes want to destroy.

"Lots of folks may not believe as we do, that Jesus was the Son of God, but pretty near everyone admires the way he lived. My son, Jesus was a true man. You can tell that by the way he forgave the people who were killing him right while they were doing it. He didn't let a whole passel of little folks pull him down to their size. He stood tall in their midst. And, Charlie, you must do the same. Maybe God made you different, but he made you special, too. Somewhere, somehow, you have just got to find love and forgiveness for those people who haven't been blessed as much as you have. Just you remember — God loves all his children. He just gives some, like you, more blessings than he does others. It's up to you to use them the right way. Now get on outside and I'll soon have supper on."

9

That was on a Monday afternoon. On Tuesday night Charlie passed his test of fire and became a man.

Shortly after he went to bed Charlie heard a knock on the door, and then he heard the deep voice of his schoolmaster requesting an audience with his mother.

Creeping to the curtain that hung in the doorway, Charlie listened as the man, all stiff and proper in his long black frock and striped pants, politely informed his mother that Charlie was no longer welcome at school. He, a decent man, simply could not tolerate such a freak in his class as Charlie was. Mrs. Langly politely thanked him for coming, saw him to the door, and then turned and collapsed on her bed, sobbing as if her heart were broken.

Timidly, Charlie approached her and placed his small hand on her arm. In anguish then she threw her arms around him and cried all the harder, while Charlie quietly waited. At last, when he was certain that he had his voice under control, Charlie spoke.

"Mom, I reckon it's just like you said. Some folks just didn't get blessed with much love, so we have to be careful of them. I can see that the schoolmaster is right, though I don't reckon he himself knows why. But it's really better if I don't go to school if my being there causes the bad to come out in others."

At that solemn pronouncement Mrs. Langly started to protest, but Charlie quickly stopped her.

"Now, Mom, don't you get to fretting. School's only good for an education, and if you'll get me the books, I reckon I can get that here at home. With your help, I expect I can teach myself most anything I need to know."

Slowly then Charlie returned to his room and

to bed. Only then, when he was certain that his mother couldn't hear him, did he finally break down and cry. It hurt, oh, it hurt so badly to be unwanted. Why were people like they were? And why did his mother have to hurt too? She wasn't a freak. The questions returned again and again, but no answer came — unless his mom was right, that they were just being tested for some great blessing. But at the time that offered but small comfort.

Thus ended Charlie's formal education, though from that Tuesday onward he grew rapidly in wisdom and knowledge. In fact, that was the beginning of a rather unusual phenomenon. As Charlie grew greater of heart, by constantly working on it, his whole personality seemed to expand. He was pleasant to everyone, cordial to friends and those not so friendly; and his smile became almost a continuous thing, even infectious to those around him. At length, when he was in his teens, there was hardly a person in the small town who did not enjoy being near Charlie. He just naturally seemed to make them feel like better individuals for being with him. It was hard to explain, but it was true. Charlie had almost become an institution.

11

Then, when he was sixteen, disaster struck. His mother, just at daylight, left the home to work in the garden. Charlie heard only the hideous screams and the heavy concussion of rifle fire. By the time he got to the backyard the Indians were only a cloud of dust fading in the distance. His mother lay in a crumpled heap, dead simply because she surprised the Indians creeping through her yard, bent on some unknown bit of mischief.

For two days Charlie grieved alone in the little home; but then on the third day he seemed to hear his beloved mother asking what had become of his great attitude.

Charles, she seemed to ask, *where is that special love that God gave you? Why, you know he loves you, and would never allow this to happen if it weren't the best for both of us. Now, get up and get busy, and let's see that smile again!*

So, with the beginnings of a smile breaking through the clouds in his heart, Charlie shuffled out the door.

The Job

After Mrs. Langly was killed, the townspeople became very concerned. In fact, they were aroused to the point that the mayor, Soren Sorensson, called a special community meeting.

Everyone tried to talk at once, but when the mayor was finally able to quiet them down he was able to learn that they had two major concerns. First, of course, was their worry about further Indian troubles. Mrs. Langly's death had been but the latest in a long series of violent Indian acts.

Second, Mayor Sorensson found to his surprise, was the townspeople's concern about Charlie. As old Jake Cracroft pointed out between chews on the quid that issued occasionally as a black jet from between his stained teeth and lips, Charlie was now alone in the world, with no kin to be looked to for help. No kin, that is, except for the whole blamed town.

"What," Mayor Sorensson asked, "are you trying to say?"

"Just this," replied George Reeves, "Charlie is pretty much a part of all of us, and I figure it's up to us to support him. Personally, I'll see that the bank gives ten dollars a month to . . ."

"Now, just hold up a bit," Jake interrupted. "I ain't talking 'bout no handouts. Don't reckon Charlie'd accept none anyways. Leastwise if I was him I certain wouldn't. I was figurin' more on some kind of a job."

"A job?" two or three echoed in surprise.

"Yeah, a job! Tarnation! I figure Charlie can work just like anyone else!"

"But, Jake, what kind of a job could a kid like Charlie do?"

"Dag-nab-it, I don't know. That's what you fellers is here for!"

As the discussion bounced back and forth, the mayor gradually stopped listening, for an idea had come to him. Charlie needed a job, and the town needed some way to be warned of the presence of Indians. What if . . .

"Folks," he suddenly said, "I think I've got it. You've been telling me we need someone to be a lookout for Indians, someone who'd do a cracker-jack job. Then you say we need to find work for Charlie. Well, I say let's hire him to be our lookout!"

15

"But he's just a kid!" Reeves shouted.

"Hang it all," Jake shouted right back, "he's the doggone oldest kid this man's ever seen. Why, in some ways I'm just a whippersnapper to the side of him. I say give 'im the job. All in favor say 'Aye!' "

Though it was most unusual and improper for a vote to be called for in such a way by such a person, there was a chorus of assenting ayes. These included George Reeves, who after a hasty glance at his peers quickly added his voice. George was, after all, a businessman first, last, and always.

And so it happened that Charlie was called into the office of the mayor, a place he had never before entered. For a few moments the mayor studied him carefully, and then he spoke.

"Charlie, we want you to know that we in this community feel a deep sorrow at the death of your mother. We also want you to know that we think an awful lot of you. For some time we've been looking for a certain individual to do a special job for us, and the townspeople feel that you are the man we need. Are you interested?"

Charlie nodded, and the mayor continued.

"Charlie, you know that Indians are a real threat to our little town, located as we are. We need a man, someone very dependable, to stand watch over our city every day from daylight until dark to warn us of possible attack. Do you think you could handle that?"

Again Charlie nodded his affirmative.

"Now, Charlie, before you accept I want you to think of one or two things. The first problem is with your walking. We feel that the best place for a lookout is on top of Baldy, just out of town. You know the hill is steep and rough. Do you think you can get to the top and back down every day?"

For the first time Charlie spoke, and as he did so his eyes blazed with determination.

"Mr. Mayor, sir, I can get to the top of old Baldy, and I will, even if I have to crawl."

The mayor smiled within himself at the pride he felt in the determination of this young man. Oh, for a son like this boy! Then he said, "Charlie, there is another thing you need to think about. If you ever see Indians we want you to build a fire to warn us. Now, if we see that fire the Indians will probably see it too. In that case there is the definite possibility that you won't get back to town before they are upon you. How do you feel about that?"

Charlie sat for a long time in silence, and Mayor Sorensson began to get uncomfortable. But still, he waited, and at last Charlie spoke.

"Sir, I don't want to die no more than anyone else. But I do want the job, and I'll do my best at it. The way Mom used to put it, if a man wasn't willing to lay his life beside his word, then his word didn't mean much. I'm mighty thankful for the job, and I've given my word I'll do it. When do you want me to start?"

17

"Tomorrow, Charlie, if you can. I'll have some of the boys haul some wood up there for you. I'll also see that you have a tent for shelter when you need it. Then each night we'll want you to report in at the sheriff's office before you go home. Can you think of anything else?"

"No, sir, and tomorrow will be fine."

"Good. And, Charlie, we'll see that you have a good salary. Plenty to live on."

"Thank you, sir."

"Thank you, Charlie. Remember, we're counting on you."

The Hill

In the predawn darkness Baldy loomed high like an ancient fortress, black and impenetrable against the star-shrouded desert sky. The hill, a steep and erratic old butte, was a little over five hundred feet in height. It had been given its name because of its vegetation-free summit. From its top one could see for several miles in any direction; the town, much less than a mile from the base of the hill, was especially in view.

Charlie stood at the hill's foot for some time, contemplating the best place to begin his climb. He tried two or three places, but each time he fell and was forced back by the steepness. At length, breathing heavily, he rested against a clump of fragrant sage. He now realized that his promise to the mayor the day before had been prophetic. If he was going to get to the top of Baldy at all, he was going to have to crawl to do it. So, on his one hand and knees he began to inch his way up the hill. In the darkness he couldn't tell the difference between a rock outcropping and a clump of prickly pear cactus, and several times the sharp spines jabbed into his hand. Because he had to hitch and pull himself upward with that one hand, it sustained great punishment, so much so that before long Charlie was sobbing in time with his labored breath and pounding heart.

At last, racked with pain, Charlie reached the rimrock, a vertical wall about ten feet high that served as his last obstacle. After pausing to get his breath, he began to climb slowly up through a small chimney or crevice he happened to find. Using his legs and back as a wedge to maintain his position, he found a handhold and inched himself up. Carefully then he located another handhold, and gradually and slowly he pulled himself up until at last he heaved his body over the top.

He lay quietly until his brain stopped swirling and his breathing was back to near normal, and then he sat up to examine the damage. His hand was torn and bloody; some of the cactus thorns were deeply embedded. His only pair of overalls were in shreds from his knees down, and his knees and legs were terribly lacerated. He had fallen so many times that they blurred together in his memory. And once, as he was sliding backward down the hill he had smacked his head so hard against a boulder that he had lost consciousness for a moment. Though the climb had been a terrible ordeal for him, Charlie allowed only one part of his brain, a small part, to complain of the agony he felt. His primary thought was of the fact that it was long past daylight, and he was late.

"Huh," he exclaimed aloud, "first day on the job, and you're not only late but you're a mess too. Boy, you got some preparing to do for tomorrow. And you got to fetch yourself up earlier too. Else climb faster. One or the other."

Charlie then set about exploring his hilltop. First of all he saw a great pile of wood near the remains of an old platform. He marveled that someone had been able to get so much of it to the top. Near the pile of wood was the small tent he had been promised and in the tent was a battered pair of army-issue binoculars.

Charlie next hobbled around the top of the hill, getting a general feeling of what he would be watching. Then he did so again, going much more slowly, examining with the binoculars each possible hiding place in the surrounding valley. He examined with care each ridge and canyon in the mountain ranges that rose both east and west of him, and he noted with interest how strategic his spot really was.

He observed also, with some surprise, that his town was actually built along the bed of a long-dry stream, that the creek that flowed through the town followed a whole new course, and was, he decided, of quite recent origin.

Charlie also discovered that from Baldy it was possible to see nearly every house in town, and with the glasses it was easy to identify most of the people as they walked up and down Main Street. For some time that first day he watched the people, and he felt a sense of exhilaration in being able to see and yet be so unobserved.

At noon Charlie ate the small lunch he had prepared. Then, during the afternoon of that first day he worked out a regular routine of patrol that he could follow so that every little while he would be able to check each point on the compass and all areas in between.

Finally, late that afternoon, he gave some attention to the sides of his hill, hoping to locate the best route for climbing. He was soon certain that there was no easy way, but the side opposite the town offered perhaps the safest path, and the rimrock on that side had large gaps in it that he could climb through. Carefully Charlie observed every foot of what was to be his trail, attempting to memorize every rock, brush, juniper, and gully that might be in his way.

With nightfall of that first day came another ordeal. Charlie was forced to crawl back down the hill, and he had to go part of the way headfirst in order to feel where he was going. The strain on his arm and shoulder was terrific. That descent was one long series of falls to the bottom, and all the cuts and bruises of that morning cried out in renewed agony. Late that evening a very sore, tired, and bloody young man shuffled into the sheriff's office to make his first report. Within twenty minutes he was in his own bed, sound asleep.

Another twenty minutes had not passed before the sheriff had related to the mayor all that he had observed. A little executive action was quickly taken, and when Charlie awoke in the morning he found on the bench near the door a new pair of overalls and a packed lunch. Then, as he stepped outside into the darkness he was immediately aware that he was not alone. Tied to the porch railing was a saddled pony. To be sure, it was an old and gentle nag, but it would provide steady and reliable transportation. On the saddle Charlie found a note, and by lamplight he read the simple message:

> First month's salary, including daily lunches, paid in advance. We surely appreciate your work.
>
> Mayor Sorensson

A tremendous feeling of love and appreciation for such wonderful people almost overcame Charlie, and he vowed, as his old horse plodded gently toward the hill, that he would never let those people down, no matter what happened.

The Rock Pile

Each day for four years Charlie spent every waking hour up on the hill. Always he was alone, and yet rarely was he lonely, for he allowed himself no time to think about it. And frequently his hill was visited, for often in the morning he would find the tracks of wandering coyote, deer, or mountain lion in the wind-rippled sand, while occasional buzzards swooped down in their circling to give closer scrutiny to the solitary figure on the rimrock.

Several times his careful observations prevented serious problems with the Indians, for with smoke to get attention and then a prearranged number of rifle shots to indicate the direction of the potential attack, he was always able to warn the townspeople to get ready.

Then, one very warm and overcast August night, Charlie crawled down the familiar trail he had worn in the hill, climbed on his horse, and made his way through the darkness into town. Tying his horse to a rail, he turned toward the sheriff's office when from out of the darkness he heard his name spoken.

Charlie turned, about to reply, when he heard another voice, and then he realized that he was not being spoken to, but about.

"Yep," the first voice was saying, "you got no need of fearing Injuns in this town. Know why? Cause we got Charlie up there on Baldy, and he always lets us know when any redskins is near."

"Charlie? I never met no Charlie in this town, and I been here three months now. You sure you ain't spinning some kind of yarn?"

"Mister, Charlie ain't no yarn. He's plain all right, and the reason you ain't met him is because he's always up on Baldy where he's supposed to be. It's his job!"

"Humph," the stranger grunted skeptically, "I guess he don't never come down neither. Right?" And he seemed to sneer as he said it.

"Why, sure he comes down. Every night, as a matter of fact, long about now."

"My friend," the stranger replied, "You'll excuse me if I don't believe you too carefully. It just ain't normal for a man to spend forever sitting on top of a hill. Yep, it's pretty tough to believe in something that don't sound no better than that."

29

With that the two men went off into the darkness, and Charlie eventually went home to bed. But sleep did not come. At first he berated himself for not having gone forward to set the record straight, or for not having at least spoken to them. But in the wee hours of the morning his thoughts took a new turn, so serious that he sat bolt upright in bed.

What if he spent his whole life up there on that hill? Why, when he finally died no one would know that he had even lived. Other men left children and families with memories of themselves, but that was out for him. What could he do?

As Charlie began his climb the next morning a light rain was falling. In the darkness his hand touched a stone that felt unlike any he had noticed before. It was as smooth as silk, but in the inky blackness of the predawn he was unable to see it.

Intrigued, he determined that he must see it. However, he knew that in order to do that he would have to carry it to the top and wait for daylight to see what kind of stone it was. Struggling with his one hand to push the stone ahead of him, Charlie made his way up the muddy slope to the top of the hill.

In the gray light of dawn it turned out to be an ordinary stone made smooth by ancient water action, but Charlie's day was spent in dreams about that stone. He dreamed of how it might have originally formed, where it had come from during its long history, and how many rivers it rolled along before it was worn down so smooth. And the thought came to him that he, himself, was like that rock, being gradually smoothed down by some pretty rough experiences along his river of life.

Darkness came so suddenly that Charlie was surprised. His day had passed more quickly than

30

any other he could remember. The next morning, in order to repeat his pleasant experience of the day before, Charlie found another unusual rock and pushed it to the top to study during the day.

For eight days this continued. Charlie studied each rock carefully, attempting to decide its composition, its origin, and its history. He then wrote in his mind a sort of textbook of geology concerning his rocks.

In the evening of the eighth day, as he bent to place his stone on top of the seven others he had brought up, he stopped in amazement. Why, there it was, the answer to his problem! His eight stones, piled four, three and one, made a little monument. He could carry a stone to the top every day, and by the time his job ended there might be quiet a pile. If nothing else, he would at least be remembered by his monument.

So Charlie began his task, and over the weeks, months, and years it became a labor of love. Each day he carefully chose a stone for his planned monument, and each day he pushed, shoved, lifted, rolled, and even dragged his stone to the top of the hill, there to place upon his growing pile, which he carefully arranged and added to so that it would not fall.

One day, when Charlie was nearly twenty-four, a whole new problem entered his life. He was sitting on the rimrock rather casually watching the town through his glasses and paying absolutely no attention to what he was seeing, when out of the bank and into his heart walked the most beautiful lady he had ever seen. He came to his feet with a lurch, and then as quickly was back down, lying on his stomach, with the glasses resting on a rock to steady them so he could see better. Quickly he revised his original opinion. He didn't think she could really be called beautiful. She was more — well, *pretty*, or *striking* was the word he wanted. Her hair gleamed like a red fire in the afternoon sun, and she walked with a ladylike and yet determined step, as though she knew exactly what she was doing and where she was going.

Too quickly she turned into a side street and was gone from his view, but try as he would, Charlie could not get her image from his mind. Through the rest of that day, all through the night, and through the next day Charlie fought his thoughts. One instant he would be thinking of her, wondering who she was and where she had come from, and the next he would be berating himself as a foolish dreamer. He just couldn't imagine why the brief glimpse of an unknown girl would affect him in such a way. Through his youth he had never allowed himself to feel an interest in girls, knowing that his deformities created obstacles that weren't worth overcoming, both for him and for any girl he might have felt an interest in. He realized that his attitude had been quite self-defeating and that perhaps he really had been feeling sorry for himself, but he had never felt that he had anything much to offer a young woman except problems.

After all, what girl would ever want to be saddled with a man so strange and deformed as he was? The very idea of himself with a girl had been so foreign that he had long ago ceased to consider and worry about it.

Now, suddenly, with no warning, he was beset with thoughts of this unknown beauty, and his mind was disturbingly unsettled.

Charlie paced his hilltop, spent extra hours studying the mountains around him, reread his few books, examined his rocks, tore down and re-stacked his growing monument, and studiously avoided any direct glance at the town—but all to no avail. And what made the agony even worse was the certainty that he would never know who she was, could never speak to her, and would never satisfy the longing that he felt to get to know her.

Several days later, as Charlie sat in the shade of his tent reading his copy of *American Antiquities*, he heard a footstep behind him where the trail came up over the top, and he turned to confront the first visitor he had ever had on his hill.

34 Clumsily he lurched to his feet to greet his guest. It was the girl! Up close she was even more lovely than she had appeared through his binoculars. Her auburn hair framed a delicate yet bold oval face, and her blue eyes danced with an excited light as she walked toward Charlie. He desperately wanted to say something, but his thoughts were in such a whirl that he found himself utterly speechless.

"Hello," she said, and Charlie noticed again how her eyes sparkled as she smiled. "I'm Nellie Reeves, and you, of course, are Charles Langly. The Great Charlie, they call you."

At this point she reached him and thrust out her hand, man-like, to shake hands with him. Charlie was surprised at the firmness of her grip, but she gave him little time to think of that, or to wonder that his thoughts could dwell upon such trivia, for laughingly she was walking away.

"So you really are a person. I wondered, you know. Charles — you don't mind if I call you Charles instead of Charlie, do you? Charles is much more refined. Good. Charles, you simply can't imagine some of the things I've heard about you since I got back to town. I've wracked my brain trying to remember you from school, and I simply haven't been able to recall a thing. Yet everyone says you've lived here all your life. So I decided to come see for myself if you were real or just some mythical creation of our imaginations.

"Oh, what a marvelous view," she continued, standing now at the edge of the hill. "Daddy — you know George Reeves, the stuffy old banker, but of course you do. Daddy said this was the best place in the whole valley for a lookout, but that I mustn't come up here. So, of course, my decision was made, and I simply had to come. Oh, Charles! I don't wonder that you stay up here every day. Look at those mountains, how that blue haze hangs in the valleys that aren't touched by the sun.

And look how golden the mountain is where the sunlight splashes on it. And feel that cool wind on your face. Oh, I love how it feels when it blows through my hair, just like when I am on a fast horse, except it is so much more quiet and serene up here."

Charles was dumbfounded. He hadn't yet said a word, and this girl, this Nellie Reeves, had carried on a whole conversation as though he had been right with her. Why, in less than five minutes she had not only made him feel quite at ease, but she had managed to show him, and to put into words, feelings he had long had but had never been able to express about the beauties of his hill.

"What a simply wonderful view you have of the town," she said. "Why, if you had some binoculars I'll bet you could even see the people."

Smiling, Charlie reached into the tent, picked up his old glasses, and shuffled over to Nellie.

"Here," he said simply. "Try them and see."

Nellie placed them to her eyes, adjusted them slightly, and gave a little squeal of pure delight.

36

"Oh, look what these do! Just look at all the people. There are Jake and old Bones whittling and chewing there in front of the hotel. And there is the widow Ames closing her laundry shop. And early too. I wonder where she is going? Look at the little boys swimming in the hole over on the creek. Wouldn't they be mortified to know that a lady was watching them?"

While she laughed in pure delight Charlie regarded her with just as pure an emotion of amazement. He had never known someone like her before, and he found himself attracted to her more and more.

For some time she watched the town, exclaiming in delight at each new event that unfolded before her. Finally she turned and handed the glasses back to Charlie.

"It's no wonder you stay up here all alone, Charles. If you ever got with people you could be the biggest gossip in town!"

Then, as she turned away, she added with a smile, "Why, I'll bet you know more about the whole bunch of us down there than we know about ourselves."

At that Charlie grinned back at her, for it was certainly true that he knew quite a bit about what went on in town. In fact, that and dreaming about his rocks were his two most enjoyable pastimes.

Then Charlie suddenly realized that it was past time to make his round of the hilltop. Pulling his eyes away from the girl, he began. Desperately he concentrated on what he was doing, forcing his thoughts together for the task. Suddenly she was there beside him, watching as he carefully scanned the country around them.

After a few minutes of silence she quietly asked him to explain what he was doing. At that Charlie, much to his surprise, found himself speaking easily and confidently to her as he told of the things he watched for, the clouds of dust or the haze that dust leaves in the air long after a rider has passed. He showed her the ravine in which he had twice before spotted Indians, and he pointed out the canyon they seemed to issue from most frequently. He also showed her the little things he loved, such as the trails the long grass made in the sand as the wind swished it back and forth, or the multicolored and multilayered lichen on the rocks. He showed her the intricate detail of a wild rosebud, and the transparent, paper-thin skin he had watched a rattlesnake shed a few weeks before. As he spoke Nellie grew more and more amazed at his insight and sensitivity.

As he spoke to her with such intentness and enthusiasm, she cautiously turned her head to study him. With a curious detachment, she realized that though she was aware of his deformities, her eyes were not drawn to them at all. Instead she found herself gazing with a feeling of almost awe at his face. And it too seemed to be a contradiction. The face was that of a young man, rather more normal looking than otherwise, and yet there was something, something . . .

Perhaps it was his eyes, but then it might have been some other feature also, for Nellie wasn't sure just what she was looking for. It was just a feeling she had, nothing more. There was something in his face that seemed to speak of great trials, of endurance gained through suffering beyond what she could even comprehend. And yet mixed with that was a look of love and compassion and sincerity that she had seen before only on the faces of little children. Just what manner of man was this Charles Langly?

For an hour they continued in this way, Charles Edward Langly, Jr., speaking easily and with great confidence to Pernella Reeves; and for the first time in his adult life Charlie was completely unconscious of the fact that he had been born different.

Then she was gone, down the trail to her horse and on her way home, and long after she was gone the sound of her laughter seemed to float in the air. And Charlie realized another first in his life that day, for as he thought of it he knew the feelings within him were true happiness.

The trail down the hill seemed much easier to Charlie that night, and though he was longer than usual getting to sleep, when he finally did so his sleep seemed much deeper and more refreshing than usual, and for a change he awoke happy and excited about going to his hill.

For several days Charlie saw no sign of Nellie, but his thoughts were never far from her. He found himself following her footprints across the hill, and often he stood and gazed at the mountains and valley, wondering at the beauty they had shared.

His thoughts were not always pleasant, however. Often as he sat he contemplated the shoulder where his arm should have been, and he became extremely conscious of the way his twisted body forced him to shuffle as he walked. More and more he castigated himself for being so foolish as to allow himself to think so much of Nellie. He grew more and more certain that her visit had been merely chance and that now her curiosity had been satisfied she would never be back.

A feeling of bitterness came with those thoughts, and it became harder than ever to appreciate all that surrounded him, as his mother had counseled him to do. He realized that these feelings were coming about because he had begun to doubt his own value, but what else could he do? How could he possibly be expected to feel good about having been given such a worthless body? What could he ever hope to offer such a wonderfully perfect person as Nellie was? How could he ever feel self-confident and have a feeling of personal worth when reality screamed so loudly at him?

Such were his thoughts as, day after never-ending day, Charlie guarded the town. Each morning he would ride to the base of the hill, fill the water tub for his horse, locate a suitable stone for his monument, struggle with it to the top of the hill, and place it carefully among the others. Then he would spend the entire day watching for sign of trouble, until with darkness he would slide down the hill and return to his little shack, there to get ready to do the same thing the next day. Often he wondered whether he could stand it much longer, and yet he kept going, simply because he knew that was what he was supposed to do.

40

Almost two weeks after Nellie's first visit to the hill she came again. And Charlie, who had almost convinced himself she would never be back, was just as surprised as before.

Nellie, always direct, spent little time with pleasantries. "Charles," she stated matter-of-factly, "Daddy told me that I must stay away from this hill, but I told him I was now a big girl and would go where I wanted and would see whomever I chose." Then she began to laugh and said, "He told me that I would become the scandal of the town. Can you imagine that? Me, who never did a bad thing in my life, being the town scandal?"

Charlie smiled with her but said nothing, for he was worrying about her father. Why had he forbidden her to come, and, even more important, why had she chosen to disobey him? Was it because of his deformities? Nellie, apparently unaware of his silence, went right on.

"Do you remember the other day, when we saw the widow Ames closing her laundry early? Well, she came in the bank yesterday, so I asked her where she was going when she closed early. Charles, you never saw anyone get so flustered and upset. She told Daddy I was a little busybody, and the uproar still hasn't ended. I told you a person could become a great gossip by being up here."

41

For a moment they stood in silence, and then Nellie spoke again.

"Charles, the quietness up here seems to get in a person. Already I have calmed down a great deal. I wish I knew what was wrong with Daddy, that he didn't want me up here. I know he isn't worried about my safety, for he lets me ride all over the valley. And I hate to be disobedient to him. That hurts me as much as it does him. I really do love him. But I do think he is wrong in this. Charles, what should I do?"

For a long moment Charlie was silent, trying to arrange his thoughts. Then at last he spoke: "I don't know, Nellie. It's been so long since I had folks that I can hardly remember. But I always tried to obey Mother, 'cause she usually knew more than me. But she did tell me that I had to think on my own and learn to do the things I thought and felt were right, even if others disagreed with me. I guess it's pretty hard to know for sure, unless you can tell by your really deep feelings."

"Well, then," she said gaily, "I'm all right. I certainly feel good about being here."

Then she turned abruptly and walked toward the monument, and Charlie's heart sank. He couldn't explain it, but somehow that monument was so special to him that he couldn't talk about it. It had become too much a part of him.

Nellie examined the pile of rocks very carefully. In the few years since Charlie had started it, the monument had grown quite large. It was now nearly as tall as Charlie, while its diameter at the base was a little over ten feet. Nellie stood and studied it for such a long time that Charlie finally walked over and sat on the rimrock. From there he could see the West Mountain, and already the blue shadows of afternoon were creeping down the canyons. Without a doubt this was his favorite view at his favorite time of day.

Suddenly Nellie was beside him, sitting on the rimrock, and Charlie waited for her burst of happy chatter. But, no, she sat in silence, apparently as enthralled with the beauty of God's handiwork as he was. For perhaps an hour they sat, communicating through silence, while the panorama of the afternoon unfolded before them.

Charlie finally spoke, and he was surprised again at how easily the words came. "Sitting here like this," he said, "watching what we've been watching, a feller sure comes to appreciate what a builder God must be. No matter how hard you look or how critical you get, there just ain't nothing done wrong."

"Yes," Nellie replied quietly, "and I'd say that you are quite a builder, too, Charles Edward Langly, Jr."

43

Surprised that she knew his whole name, Charlie turned a questioning glance on her. "A builder? What've I ever built?"

"Oh, stuff!" Nellie responded indignantly. "You know as well as I do. But if you want to play dumb, I'll go along with you. Most obvious, of course, is your pile of rocks back there."

He couldn't understand it, but when Nellie called his monument a pile of rocks Charlie suddenly felt hurt. Why did something that was so special to him appear so common to another, such as Nellie.

She, in turn, couldn't help but notice his expression, and she suddenly knew that she had made some sort of blunder.

"Oh, Charles, I've hurt you. What did I say wrong?"

"Well," and Charles fought for control, "nothing, really. I guess I'm just a little touchy today."

"That's not so. Please tell me. I really wish you would."

For a time Charlie wondered just how to tell her, but at last he just blurted it out. "Nellie, them rocks is my monument."

"Oh," she replied thoughtfully. "I knew they were special simply because they had been placed so carefully. But I didn't expect them to be that special. Charles, tell me about it. Please?"

"Well, I reckon there ain't too much to tell," he replied evasively, alarmed now that he had exposed himself so much. "It's just a pile of rocks I've been making."

Nellie searched his face for a long moment before quietly replying. "I guess maybe I deserved that, Charles. I really don't have any business asking these questions. I won't pry any more."

Of course, that made Charlie feel worse than ever. He so wanted to share with her his feelings. Next to his mother, Nellie had become the most special person he had ever known, and he hadn't meant to hurt her. Maybe, maybe she could understand. At least, he decided, it was worth a try.

"Nellie, look at me. Tell me honestly: what do you see?"

"I see *you*, Charles."

"Yes, I know, but I don't mean that, and you know it. You see the way I am. What can I ever hope to offer anyone in this life? Nothing! And since I have nothing to offer, when I am gone, there will be nothing left for people to remember me by."

"And so," she said quietly, and Charles silently wondered at the tear coursing down her cheek, "you are building your own monument, to make certain you are never forgotten."

"That's right!" he replied with conviction. "Each day I pick a rock for the pile, and each day it grows a little larger. One day all the valley will be able to see it, and they will always know that I have been here."

Nellie sat silently for so long after he finished speaking that Charlie grew nervous. Gradually the shadows lengthened across the top of the hill, and at last the lowering sun disappeared behind the mountain.

That seemed to awaken the girl, for she jumped to her feet, took Charlie's hand in hers, squeezed

45

it, and thanked him for a wonderful afternoon. Then she was gone.

Long after he had retired to bed Charlie was still rehearsing in his mind his conversation with Nellie, and the more he thought about it the worse he felt. Oh, if he could only live the day over again. He would never expose himself as he had done. She now knew how foolish he really was, and her imagined laugh of ridicule seemed to ring in his ears. Why, the idea of his monument now seemed awfully foolish even to him. His last thought before finally going to sleep was that his monument had grown as large as it ever would. It was finished.

Shortly before noon the next day he heard the familiar footsteps, and there she came over the rim as happy and bubbly as ever. She walked straight to him, took his arm, and led him to their place on the rimrock. Then she told him to sit down with her.

"Charles," she said, "I've something to say, and I want you to listen carefully."

"Yesterday, when you told me that you were building your monument, the idea seemed so strange and unusual that I couldn't accept it. I wanted to laugh, or cry, or I don't know what. I just couldn't believe you were really serious. The idea seemed so, well, so morbid, I guess."

Charlie, at this frank and honest confession, felt his ears and neck turn red with shame and humiliation. Why had he ever been so stupid and foolish as to . . .

"When I left yesterday, Charles, that was all I could think about. Last night was pretty rough for me because I felt terrible about what I'd done. But I want to tell you about what happened to me. On my way into town some of the boys stopped me and started teasing me about coming up here to see you. Or at least they were teasing me until the Adams boy, oh, what is his name . . . ?"

"Joseph."

"That's right, Joseph Adams. He rode up and told the other fellows to beat it, and they did. Just like that. And do you know what he did then? He told me a story, a story of a little boy thrown from a horse and lying in the sagebrush bleeding to death and unable to move because of a terribly broken leg. Then a man came, a tremendously strong man with only one arm and hand. He used that one hand as a tourniquet while he carried the little boy on his twisted back clear into town where he could be helped. Joseph Adams told me that the man who helped him was probably the best man he had ever known."

47

Charlie remained silent. Funny, but he'd forgotten all about that afternoon when he'd found that little kid thrown from his horse. He recalled wistfully how his own horse had become frightened upon seeing him carrying such a burden, and how long and painful that walk into town had been. There were times, he remembered, when he felt he wasn't going to make it.

"Nellie, anybody'd have done that. I just saw him from the hill and . . ."

"Wait a minute, Charles. I'm not through. When I got home last night Daddy gave me a real Scotch blessing, and he said some pretty cruel things about you. I've never seen Daddy like that, and it really hurt me to hear it. But the important thing is that while he was yelling at me and saying those horrible things, I suddenly knew that you had been all through that many times before, that you had been hurt deeply by the cruelty and ignorance of others, and that somehow you had risen above it.

"Charles, that was when I realized what your monument meant, and from then on I couldn't get you off my mind. Let me tell you what I decided, and please don't interrupt. All right?

"All your life you have been growing and over-coming. For most of the rest of us life has been simply a matter of getting older, while for you it has involved the necessity of surviving and grow-ing *up*.

48

"Now, don't think I'm silly, please, but I can see how your monument is really an outward reflection of your life. Each rock you bring up this hill could be like one more quality you have added to your character."

Charlie was bewildered, and it must have shown in his expression, for Nellie quickly con-tinued, "Charles, what you have done and are

doing now is simply wonderful. Don't you see that? When you saved Joseph Adams you added the stones of compassion and sacrifice to your character, while each time you are insulted and ridiculed you find a way to add a stone of forgiveness. Oh, Charles, it's all so plain to me. Now I finally know why I just couldn't keep away from your hill and away from you."

Suddenly Nellie began to weep, and Charlie, like all men before and since, found himself completely at a loss. There was just nothing to say, so he simply put his arm around her and held her close, while her crying grew more intense. And the thought crossed his mind, as he was holding her, that he had just added the stone of true love to his monument. Smiling then, Charlie couldn't help but wonder at how simply and beautifully Nellie had shown him his life. How could someone be as special as she was?

50

The Monument

The years passed quickly by, and with each day Charlie's monument grew. Yet the years were not easy, and frequently he and Nellie experienced severe trials.

Such an experience occurred on their wedding day when everyone in town attended the wedding but George Reeves, Charlie's new father-in-law. Charlie had been so angered at the hurt and pain Nellie experienced that he hurled his chosen rock with all his might into the side of his monument the next time he climbed the hill.

The resulting chaos had taken him three days to rebuild, and Nellie, bless her heart, had reprimanded him for his pride and anger. When Charlie finally saw through her frown and into the twinkle of her eyes he laughed with her and suddenly realized how good his new wife was going to be for him.

Charlie was able to help Nellie, too. Rumor upon rumor spread abroad as to why such a girl as she would stoop to marry a strange and crippled man like Charlie. And many of the old wags in

53

town held their noses in the air and turned away whenever Nellie approached. Though this hurt her terribly, she never mentioned it to Charlie. Yet he seemed to know of it and to understand her feelings, for he often spoke to her of the qualities of calmness and serenity. Over and over he told her that as an individual develops inner strength and confidence his need for the praise of other people diminishes.

He described to her what he called his inner citadel, a fortress he could retreat into when the world became too rough for him to handle. That fortress was built up of self-confidence and a strong feeling of his own personal worth, two qualities he was still working to develop more fully. However, he told her, the outward reflections of that inner citadel were calmness and serenity.

So Nellie tried to ignore the crude comments that occasionally came to her ears in town, and though she was not immediately successful, she did find that over the years she gradually improved.

54

One good thing was brought about by all of this, however. Nellie spent less and less time in town and more and more time on the hill with Charlie, and over the years this caused them to grow very close to each other. Besides being husband and wife, each of them became the other's best friend and confidant.

One day Nellie calmly announced to Charlie that she was expecting a child. The poor man immediately got so excited that Nellie couldn't help but laugh and repeat his own preaching on calmness. Charlie accepted her teasing and then became so overly solicitous that Nellie practically had to plead to be allowed to climb the hill after that.

Finally, after nine everlastingly long months, there came a child, a beautiful little daughter who was given the name of Anna. She was the light of their lives and the pride of their hearts, and the two parents were amazed at how much happier they were with her in their home than they had been before. They had never guessed that children could bring so much joy.

Suddenly, little Anna grew pale and weak, and in just days the dreaded typhoid had taken her from them. Charlie and Nellie found their grief to be almost unbearable, and for days all work on the monument ceased; Charlie just couldn't bring himself to go to the hill.

Oh, how lonely death was! They constantly found their eyes wandering to the little crib, and each time they did so they experienced a new shock. Little Anna was really gone, and it was oh so hard to accept.

They told themselves that she was happier up in heaven, and they truly believed that she was. Still, the loneliness was almost unbearable, and forever they seemed to be waiting to hear her happy little cry from out in the yard. If they had experienced tests before, Anna's death was their trial by fire.

At last, though, Charlie returned to his hill. In his agony of spirit he dragged a huge stone to the top and carefully placed it at the bottom of his monument. It was a terrific ordeal for him to get it to the top, yet somehow the effort made him feel better and he was able to face life once again with a smile.

One day as Nellie sat watching the town she had an idea which she immediately expressed to Charlie. Since they had no one else to share their love with, why not share it with the whole town? Charlie couldn't see a way to do that, so with little acts of compassion Nellie set about showing him.

From the top of the hill she would watch the little town for hours, choosing each day someone who might need or want their help. Then that help or service would be given secretly so the beneficiary would never know who had helped him.

Occasionally a real problem was observed, such as when Charlie spotted smoke coming from under the eaves of Mrs. Ames's laundry. He was able to alert the town so that the fire was put out before it did much damage.

The widow Ames, up to then their staunch enemy, made a special trip to their hill to thank them. As they spoke together she suddenly broke down and wept with gratitude that these two whom she had treated as enemies with the lies she had spread would have helped her anyway.

Charlie and Nellie were both genuinely amazed, and said so. How could they or anyone else have ever considered doing otherwise? From that day on the widow Ames was perhaps their most loyal and staunch friend.

Mostly, though, in their efforts to secretly share their love with the town, they just did "trivial" things. Sometimes in the morning they would leave a loaf of warm bread on someone's doorstep, or Nellie might send Charlie out to "steal" someone's laundry when it was left out overnight. In the morning the "victim" would find the laundry neatly pressed and stacked on his doorstep, with absolutely no indication of where it had spent the night.

These and other similar acts of kindness brought great joy and happiness to their lives; lives made so empty by the loss of their lovely daughter.

Soon Nellie was expecting again, but she was having problems this time; so Charlie was once again alone on the hill. But with a new child coming, how could he feel badly about that?

Then came the day when a rapidly approaching horseman gave Charlie a strange foreboding of trouble. Anxiously he slid down the hill to meet the man, and when the grim message was received all haste was made. Yet even then Charlie was too late. When he got home his beloved Nellie was gone, and her baby, a beautiful little boy, was gone with her. Charlie was alone once more, and it was due, so everyone who had been there said, to the mistakes of the drunken doctor who attended her.

For weeks Charlie was numb. He kept his lonely vigil on the hill, but his monument grew no higher. In fact, the only thing that seemed to grow was his hatred for the doctor who had killed his wife and child.

Then one afternoon as he sat on the rim of the hill he noticed that extra heavy rain clouds were boiling around the peaks to the north. Watching through his binoculars he suddenly realized that a tremendous wall of water, a flash flood, was sweeping down the old gully toward the town.

Charlie slid down the hill to his horse and began a mad dash to town, shouting the warning as he went. Once his horse stumbled, and Charlie was certain that he'd never get to town on time. But he urged his horse up and onward, and soon he had the satisfaction of seeing the last of the people struggle to higher ground. The dust raised by the rushing water could be seen as Charlie, looking back one last time, felt his heart sink within him. On the hotel steps lay a man apparently unable to move further.

The thought, *you can't make it,* flashed through his mind, but then his horse wheeled and he was going back. As he drew nearer, though, he suddenly recognized the man. It was the doctor, drunk as usual.

Charlie almost turned back, feeling exultant that the doctor was finally going to get what he de-

served. But then, with a savage curse, he sawed the reins and pulled his horse near the porch. No matter what the man had done, Charlie could not let him drown.

The race was close, and many who remembered Nellie's death watched in wonder as Charlie risked his life for one he detested so badly. Finally both, though thoroughly wet, were safe, and Charlie, to his own wonderment, was experiencing a real feeling of concern for this despised individual.

The next day, as Charlie climbed his hill, he once again pushed a stone before him. And in his mind he could see Nellie, her eyes flashing in merriment, expressing approval of his renewed work. His monument would continue to grow.

The years came and went, and not always were Charlie's efforts successful. The last Indian problems occurred right under Charlie's nose, so to speak, and yet he was unaware of it at the time.

A hue and cry was raised for his dismissal, and Charlie experienced again the bitter taste of failure as he carefully wrote out his resignation.

But cooler heads prevailed; Charlie was encouraged by a wise and benevolent town council; and his job on the hill continued.

With this experience too came new growth, and he made a secret resolve to be more alert and to do a better job than he had been doing. In time his desire for excellence became almost a passion, and through the years he constantly taught himself new skills and habits.

Finally, one day when Charlie was quite old, he rode slowly to the base of his hill. He had long since stopped watching for Indians. He now watched for people and for floods, in that order of importance, and he was kept employed by the town for that purpose. Hardly a day went by that someone didn't come to see either him or his monument, and he always looked forward to their visits. Good friends, he had learned, were of high priority in a happy life, and so he carefully cultivated friendships with everyone he possibly could.

On this morning it took him a long time to find the rock he wanted, and still longer to get it up the hill. While he was climbing, the thought came to him that Nellie would have a name for this rock just like she had so frequently those many years before.

Finally reaching the top, he leaned far over, clutched the rock tightly, and then quickly straightened, throwing the rock up as high as he could unto the monument. He listened for a moment as it clattered to a stop, and then he shuffled around to his tent, picked up his glasses, and went along the old trail to Nellie's seat on the rimrock. It was here that he spent nearly every day, for beneath the rimrock, on the slope of the hill, lay the graves of his wife and children. It was his favorite spot on the hill.

But today everything seemed different. Today it seemed to Charlie that Nellie sat beside him, and so, as on other special occasions, he began to talk to her.

"Well, Nellie, what do you think of our monument now? Pretty big, ain't it? That'll learn you for laughing at me. See how it covers pretty near the whole dang top here, and I reckon it's at least twenty or thirty feet high. Yep, it's getting big. I'm kinda proud of it." Off and on through the morning old Charlie continued his conversation, and when he wasn't talking he was looking and watching.

"Nellie, ain't it still a beautiful view from up here? Look at how them folks down there are spreading out, farms all over the place. Why, it beats all I ever heard of. Who'd of ever thought that sage flat down there could be farmed?

"And, hey, look at how the sun hits here where Anna and little Charlie and you are buried. I'll bet you like that, don't you?

"And, say, Nellie, there come those blue shadows of yours down those canyons over there. Gosh, but I love those beautiful shadows. Fact is, Nellie, God sure did give us a beautiful world. I'm right thankful for it. By the way, you and me added maybe our best rock to the old pile today.

I've decided to call it our gratitude rock, 'cause I've felt so doggone thankful lately for all the good Lord has done for us. Fact is, Nellie, I'm hopin' that right soon I can tell Him 'Thank you,' in person."

For a few minutes longer Charlie watched the blue shadows creep down the valley and then gradually up toward his monument. At last he closed his eyes and relaxed a little. Then suddenly

he sat bolt upright and rubbed his eyes in amazement. No! It couldn't be! He blinked his eyes rapidly, again and again, but it did no good. For there, coming up the old trail toward him, was his beloved Nellie, as fresh and beautiful as ever. Quickly she crossed the top of the hill, and as she drew nearer Charlie could see the same old twinkle in her eyes.

"Well," she asked in her petulant way, and Charlie actually jumped at the sound of her voice. He still wasn't certain this was real.

"Charles Edward Langly, Jr., I declare! What kind of a gentleman are you, sitting there in the presence of a lady?"

Alarmed and embarrassed Charlie jumped to his feet, and only then did he realize that she was teasing him, and a slow grin spread across his face as he held out his hand to her.

"Nellie, what in . . . ?"

"Hush, Charles, I'll answer all your questions in a minute. Now stand still and let me look at you."

Numbly Charlie watched her as she stood, chin in hand, and studiously regarded him, her gaze going from his head to his feet. To say Charlie was confused would have been a gross understatement.

"I declare," she said at length. "I always thought so; I even said it would be so — but until now I was never certain. I'm happy to know I was right."

"Nellie, what on earth are you talking about?"

"Charles, what an awful joke. But to answer your question, of course I am talking about you, about your arms and legs. You don't look one whit better with two arms and straight legs than you did before. I always told them it wouldn't make a bit of difference. Now come on. You simply can't sit dreaming on the edge of this hill forever."

Charlie just stared at her, his mind in a daze. Then Nellie took his hand and led him off the hill, and he had only a moment to wonder at the ease with which he moved and at the other arm swinging freely at his side. Quickly then he glanced back, and he wasn't surprised at all to see himself lying quietly on the rimrock, apparently asleep, with a happy smile of relief and anticipation on his face.

The years have come and gone, and anyone in the little town will, if asked, explain proudly how the giant old monument came to be on top of Baldy. And the story will involve the tale of how old Charlie built it, one day and one rock at a time, right up to the day of his death.

But if a visitor is lucky enough to ask one of Joseph Adams's children or grandchildren, or one of the many descendants of a reformed drunken doctor, or perhaps one of the countless descendants of dozens of others helped by crippled old Charlie and his lovely wife, Nellie, that visitor will hear an entirely different story.

Yet it, too, will be the story of Charlie's Monument.

The Story Behind the Book

Many people have wondered how Charlie's Monument *came into being. We approached the author with this question, and this is his story.*

In 1974 I taught a class of seminary students who, collectively, seemed to have the lowest self-esteem of any students I had ever taught. They felt that life had dealt with them unfairly, and they were quite certain that, no matter what they tried to do, it would end in at least partial failure. I worked with them for the entire school year, and, as far as I could tell, made no headway at all. One afternoon after having spent an hour or so in my office with several of them, I went home feeling very depressed and ineffective.

My wife, Kathy, and I had prayed much about the problem. We did so again that evening, and then we retired. For several hours I tossed and turned, finally arising at about 4:00 A.M. to go to the seminary. Once there I tried to prepare a lesson but I couldn't; so I spent the remainder of the morning on my knees pleading for help. By 8:30 when my first class started I not only had not received any answers, but neither did I have a lesson prepared, which was a dangerous situation for that particular class.

After the devotional I arose, fully intending to open the class to a general discussion of theological principles. But when I began speaking, instead of hearing what I had intended to say I heard myself uttering the words: "Charlie's mother, when she first saw her tiny boy, held him close and cried just a tiny bit."

It is difficult to describe the feelings I had then, and equally difficult to describe the experience itself. As the story of a little crippled boy unfolded, I found myself listening as intently as any of my students, and I vividly recall the emotions and tears we all shared at each new development in his life. The story ended just as the class period did, but no one moved. We all seemed to feel that we had shared a very unusual and special hour together; and in the days and weeks that followed, I could see that there had indeed been a change in the attitudes of the students.

Throughout that day I related the story to all of my classes; and when school ended I ran to my office, limbered up my three typing fingers, and went to work typing out what I had learned. I then made a copy and sent it to my brother Brenton, who was teaching seminary in Arizona. He read it to his classes and had similar experiences with his students. And so we determined to use it each year as our special lesson.

But word of the story spread. One evening I was visiting with a lady about the story, and she suggested that I make a book of it. Because my father, Gayle Yorgason, had challenged me to one day write a book that contained something of substance, the woman's suggestion intrigued me. The trouble was, the story was too short for a book, and I couldn't imagine how to change it, though I tried unsuccessfully several times to lengthen it.

Then one night, just as I was going to bed, an idea came. I grabbed my pencil and a pad of paper and commenced writing. At 7:15 the next morning I was finished. My wife typed the expanded version, and with great expectations I mailed it to an eastern publisher. By 1976 I had repeated the process over twenty times, each time with a similar result: Thanks, but no thanks. The story is too short or too this or that or not enough this or that. All I had for my efforts was an impressive stack of rejection slips and two dog-eared copies of the story. Totally discouraged, I quit trying to find a publisher.

A few weeks later I was sitting in my office when I had a very strong impression to take the manuscript to Ricks College Press. Without too much hesitation I did so, asked (no, persuaded), the Press to store the manuscript for me, and returned to the seminary. A week later school ended, and I took my family on a short trip. The morning after we returned, the Teton Dam broke.

The next time I saw the seminary site, the building and all its contents had been destroyed by water and mud. Our home was also flooded, and several weeks passed before I happened to think of my manuscript sitting high and dry at the college. As I recalled why I had taken it to the college, and as I contemplated the fact that all else I owned was ruined, I felt certain that that manuscript had been preserved for a reason. So the next day I went to the college Press and asked them to print two hundred copies of *Charlie's Monument*. They laughed and told me they wouldn't do less than a thousand at the unit price I wanted. I gulped, told them to proceed, and wondered what I would ever do with a thousand books.

One day, I told my dad that I was having *Charlie's Monument* published (it was being typeset). He asked me why I didn't use the real names of the people, since I was going to print it. Surprised, I asked what he meant. "Your grandparents," he replied. "That is the story of your grandparents." Somewhat taken aback, I considered dad's statement and for the first time realized that my story was indeed similar to theirs. Grandfather, whom I remembered very little about, had been born crippled (though not quite so severely as Charlie).

That was enough for me. Hastily I called the Press and asked them to change names, which they willingly did — the woman became Nellie, my grandmother's name. They had already printed the cover, however, so it was too late to change Charlie's name.

The book, a little yellow paperback, came out in November, 1976, and the first printing was sold out within a few days. I ordered another two thousand, hardcover this time, and they were gone by Christmas. So then I ordered more.

Meanwhile, Brenton had written a manuscript which had been accepted for publication by Bookcraft. One day he took a copy of *Charlie's Monument* to them and suggested that they reconsider it. They did so, repented of their previous decision, took over publication rights; and the book has continued from there.

This, however, is not the end of the story. In January, 1978, dad and I were in Sanpete County, Utah, visiting with an older man about area folklore. During the conversation he and dad casually began to discuss my grandfather, and this gentleman asked if we had ever heard why grandfather had quit school. Surprised, I shook my head; I didn't even know he had quit school. I was then told a fascinating story. One day when grandfather was in the third grade his teacher became angry over something, called him a freak, and made him stand on his bad leg in the corner all day. When that day ended grandfather walked out of the schoolroom door and never returned. The incident was indeed sad, but what made my head reel was the remarkable similarity between my grandfather's experience and what I had written about Charlie.

A little later, as we were leaving, the old gentleman asked if we knew about the rock monuments grandfather had built on the mountaintops in the area. Neither of us did. And almost hesitantly, fearing for some reason what I felt certain I was going to hear, I asked if he happened to know why grandfather had built them.

"Sure," he said, "he told me once he built them so folks would know that he'd been there." Again the similarities were staggering; and so, literally, was I.

As we rode home, dad and I talked about my grandparents, and I made a mental list of the similarities between their lives and the lives of Charlie and Nellie in my story. Both grandmother and Nellie were ridiculed and later ostracized for marrying a cripple. Two of my grandparents' children, a boy and a girl, died. The boy died at birth, and the girl passed away at a very young age, as Charlie and Nellie's children had died in the story. Both my grandfather and Charlie struggled with the problem of low self-esteem, each feeling that, because he was not physically whole, neither could he be wholly a man. They both lived their lives in the mountains, neither achieved worldly recognition, both were lonely, and both in their loneliness did little things for people to show they cared. Finally there was the fact that both were crippled, both were called freaks by their schoolteachers before quitting school, and both built rock monuments so people would one day know that they had existed.

In the early summer of 1978, I received a call from a man asking how much of the story was true. I told him what I knew and asked why he wanted to know. He then told me of a large rock monument on top of a mountain above his ranch in Sanpete County. After some hasty arrangements the next morning, he and I rode to the monument on horses. How can I describe my feelings as I dismounted and examined the monument, a man's effort to tell others that he had once been alive? In the area were aspen trees upon which was carved grandfather's brand, the quarter-circle Y, and so I knew he had indeed been there. Of course it is simply speculation as to whether he built that exact monument, but it is possible that he did. He was there as a sheepherder and certainly could have.

Now I sit back and consider. The list of similarities between my grandfather and Charlie is impressive and to me it seems to go far beyond coincidence. More than ever, I am convinced that

I myself did not write the story of *Charlie's Monument*. Rather, it was given to me. I wonder if perhaps grandfather, who lived and died thinking of himself as a total failure, a man good for nothing but herding sheep and building rock monuments, might not have been allowed to work through his grandson in sharing his life — sharing so that others might learn the vital lessons about self-esteem which he never learned during mortality.

Could it be? I think so.